TELEMARKETERS BE GONE

How To Guide
to Defeating the Annoyance
of Phone Calls from Telemarketers!

Charmaine Trofin

&

Melinda Devine

Drawings by Fern Devine,
Charmaine Trofin & Melinda Devine
Edited by Beverley Kroeker

Special Thanks to our Family
for their Support and Encouragement

Dedication

This book is dedicated to Aunt Sally who shares her Love and Homemade cookies with her many nieces and nephews! She's an inspiration to us all.

Introduction

Throughout the years, family, friends and I have discussed how frustrating telemarketers can be and how annoying it is when you have your hands full and someone phones you in the privacy of your own home. They ask you if you want to purchase something or buy into an amazing new scheme; or tell you that you are the winner of a once-in-a-lifetime opportunity!

Well, we sat down and discussed solutions to this nuisance – and not only are these solutions effective, they are hilarious and entertaining for the listener (telemarketer). These techniques are proven to turn a potentially negative situation into a positive one that can have an enjoyable ripple effect for all.

Important! – always remember to say immediately that you are house sitting – then continue with the choices that are outlined in this manual. To increase its effectiveness, it is best to keep it on your person or near the phone at all times. Or – best case scenario – practice and memorize the responses so to increase the impact. On many a cold night here in Canada we have role-played these scenarios and laughed to our hearts' content!

Most importantly – feel the character, be the telemarketer, be the customer –

FEEL IT, LIVE IT, BE IT!

Here is an example of an actual conversation between you and the soon-to-be entertained telemarketer:

Telemarketer: "Good evening, this is Ted's Carpet Cleaning. We have a special offer this week only, for carpet cleaning in your home."

You: "I am sorry but I am housesitting. Actually, the owners of the house have gone to Persia to test carpets – they are searching for the magic carpets that fly – because the airlines keep increasing their fares. They aren't expected back for 10 years, but I can certainly take your name and number and if you wish, I will phone you at home ASAP should you wish to purchase one."

See how this role reversal has turned a negative situation into a beautiful expression of humanity?

On the next pages you will find the materials that will help you to begin your conquest of fending off the plea of Telemarketers. Use them as you wish!

☎ Gone to NASA to build a ladder tall enough to reach the planet Pluto to prove beyond a shadow of a doubt whether or not it is a planet. Expected back in about 23.5 years.

Here I Come, Pluto! One Nail at a Time!

☎ Gone to Russia to search for a rare egg, painted by the chicken that may have laid it. They will be back in ten years.

☎ Gone to the jungle to taste-test exotic plant life to discover which plants are poisonous – depending on the results, they may or may not return.

☎ Gone to Romania to research Vampires to see if they are related to the leech family.

☎ Gone to Sweden to search for the Abominable Snowman, they'll be back in 6 years.

☎ Gone to the Alps to yodel within the depths of the mountains and valleys; to find the quintessential spot for the most impeccable yodeling. This may take decades – I hope they do not succumb to an avalanche because of their yodeling efforts.

☎ Gone to Italy to make a bridge out of pasta – back in 16 years.

☎ Gone to Peru to make enough Alpaca sweaters to clothe the world. Be back in 30 years.

☎ They have gone to join the circus. The wife always dreamed of being the bearded lady and the husband wanted to make her dreams come true.

☎ Gone to Californian to try out a solar powered surfboard that may travel forever – not expected to return.

☎ Gone to find the pot of gold at the end of the rainbow – but they keep finding the pot full of nothing but Leprechaun poop! They refuse to give up their quest; these Leprechauns eat tons of fiber and are a tricky bunch.

☎ Gone to Egypt to see how many Asps are left. They may be back in 10 years – or not – depending whether they have been bitten by one!

☎ Gone to Drumheller to sit on a dinosaur egg. They must remain seated in a posed position until the egg hatches – an estimated 45 years. Boy, the world had better watch out, EH!

☎ Gone to the Middle East to see if it is actually in the middle. They brought their ruler with them. May take 60 years to calculate.

☎ Gone to Australia to see if the Platypus actually knows what it is? They became obsessed about this. They spent most of their life savings on researching this and finally made the decision to just travel there and ask them in person. Will never return.

☎ Gone to Greece to erect a sculpture out of broken dishes. Will be back in 14 years.

☎ Gone diving in the Atlantic Ocean to look for loose change, never to return. Last month they only found 10 cents. The sharks are getting agitated.

☎ Gone to Florida to study flamingos and determine if they understand the benefits of standing on one foot. Believed that they are the true Masters of Yogi. Soon to be named Yogi Flamingo! You are the first to know this information; please don't share – the owners of the house have sworn me to secrecy.

☎ Gone to Asia to count individual rice grains in the largest rice paddy in the world. Not expected to return till 2041.

☎ Gone to France to see if wearing a beret
will inspire artistic creativity

☎ Gone to Colombia to test a rare coffee
that may help with sleep apnea.

☎ Gone to Spain to run with the bulls and
may return – depending on how well they
can zig when the bulls and zag.

☎ Gone to England to research the theory that Queen Bees and Royalty have a blood line interrelated through proof blood quantum. Will take years to research since both the bees and Royalty are rather busy.

☎ Gone to Jaipur and on to the Thar Desert
to find a mirage that looks like a fast food
restaurant that sells slushies and ice.

☎ Gone to Ireland in search of Leprechauns and Fairies, for it is believed that they interbred and are now called Leprefairies. I received a letter in the mail from them the other day and they have actually been bitten by the Leprefairies and are suffering greatly; one has succumbed to the bite. I live in fear every day that the Leprefairies might make their way to Canada.

☎ Gone to Scotland to recreate a kilt that spins while playing the bagpipes.

☎ Gone to Kalamazoo to float on a canoe to see if the chickamagoo actually exists. I googled it the other day – it said it didn't. I swear they are never coming back!

☎ Gone to Iceland to check the volcanic activity. May be back in five years – depends whether the volcano erupts or not.

☎ Gone to Taiwan to see how things are made.

☎ Gone to Tibet to search for a rare mushroom cure for moments that you cannot get back – like this one right now. I truly hope they find the mushrooms soon. Not expected back for 15 years.

☎ Went on a trek to the West Indies to gather as many grains of sand as possible; counting and tossing the ones that aren't a perfect sphere.

☎ Gone to Timbuktu in search of a rare tissee bug. It is said that they bake seeds in their mouths which causes a chemical reaction and produces natural healing essences in the environment. Instead of aromatherapy it will be called bug-a-therapy.

☎ Gone to area 51 to research aliens in their new habitats; may be back – or not – depends whether the aliens are friendly.

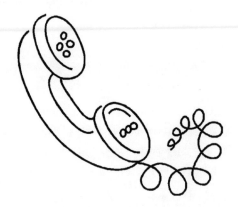

☎ Gone to the North Pole with a bunsen burner to see how long it will take to melt an iceberg.

☎ No, last night they were having a BBQ and all of a sudden a bright beam of light shot from the sky. I went to get the lemonade. When I returned they had disappeared and when I searched for them all I saw was ashes and their burnt and steaming shoes. I think aliens do exist – I am terrified! Are you an alien?

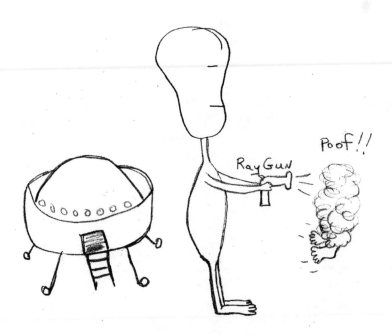

☎ Gone to Holland to join a clog dancing group. Never coming home for they are finally living their dreams!

☎ Gone to Hollywood – hopefully to hit the big time in a hotdog commercial.

☎ Gone to Italy to see if crushing grapes with athlete's foot will produce a wine that will make you more active.

☎ Gone to Egypt to find the truth behind the "Mummy's Curse"!!

☎ Gone to Phoenix to rattle snakes.

☎ Gone to Hawaii to plant seeds in a hula dancer's waist in hopes of developing a hula skirt that can grow grass and will only need a weed eater to trim it.

☎ Gone to find the underwater Atlantis in search of the answer to why certain materials can last millennia in the water.

☎ Gone to farm country, investigating whether giving vinegar to chickens will produce a pickled egg.

☎ Gone to Mexico in search of a jumping bean which can be entered as an Olympic competitor in pole vaulting.

☎ Gone to walk barefoot across the North Pole to see how long it will take before their feet fall off.

☎ Gone to Nashville to listen to music and try to break the world record for number of tears it takes to fill a bucket.

☎ Gone on a mission to visit all the stores in the world – they just love shopping and getting deals – they're not coming home until every store has been visited, it will take the rest of their lives.

☎ Gone to tip-toe through the woods to see if any wildlife will notice.

☎ Gone to the forest to determine once and for all – if a tree falls and no one is around to hear it, does it make a sound? Although it may take a long time since they actually will be there to hear it. Not expected to return!

☎ Gone to teach ants how to build structures that would be useful in OUR world!

☎ Gone to find out how a berry can be combined with straw to make an edible fruit. The next phase of the research is to gather stats on whether cows or humans prefer the product. They have already been away for six months and not expected back for another eight.

☎ Went away for a few years to find a needle in a haystack. Have no idea when they are coming back.

☎ Gone to stroll around the world without funds to see how generous people can be! They have already been gone for 4 years, so the world is more generous than I thought – I don't think they'll be back for many more years.

☎ Went trekking through the most treacherous bush country to see if bears and cougars will be disturbed. If they are, the next test is to see if they will eat them. The final test is how fast they can run – they may never return!

☎ Went to develop an invisible phone; the trick will be to find it once it's made!

☎ Gone to Mongolia to learn how to hunt with eagles. May be back in 50 years if learning to flap arms is as easy as it looks. Phone back in the summer of 2064.

☎ Gone to Holland to count the tulips. I just received a post card in which they said the count so far was 110,118 and they have only been there a week. Estimated to be back in about 5 years.

☎ Left to go on a turtle race around the world. Have been gone for months already and have only travelled 3000 kilometers – another 40,008 to go! It'll take years – you should join them and cheer them on!

☎ Went to LEGOLAND in California to count every Lego block. Return date unknown.

☎ Went in search of Atlantis to discover the beginning of the human race. May never return.

☎ Gone to Russia – possibly moved there – to learn how to build the Onion Domes on the churches. They'll first have to learn to speak Russian, then how to build, and also what the architecture is all about.

☎ Gone to Papua, New Guinea to research whether there are guinea pigs living there and if they are all Papas. No idea when they will be back.

☎ Gone to England to have "high tea" with the Queen; then to travel the Silk Road by camel. Not expected to return for several years.

☎ Went to Ottawa to observe the House of Commons and watch the Senate proceedings. Will return when the politicians start making sense. I have concluded they will never return home. EVER!

☎ Went to follow their dreams and work at a remote ranch in Northern Alberta. There are no phones, no computers and not even a mailing address.

☎ Gone to Italy to learn the art of making Pizza. They told me it will take a minimum of twenty-five years.

☎ They invented a time machine and have gone back to Prehistoric times. Don't tell anyone but they are bringing back a T-Rex. I fear for our future!

☎ They went to the forest to study the behavior of rabbits. Now they can no longer speak English! They spend all day bouncing around and chewing on the furniture. I don't know what to do – they eat 150 pounds of vegetables a day! I think I will have to surrender them to the SPCA.

☎ Gone to Vatican City to meet with the Pope and discuss the meaning of life. Not sure if they will ever return.

☎ Gone to Idaho to figure out why they got famous for the world's most famous potatoes. May take years to test every potato on every farm!

☎ Gone to find the Yeti Crab that disappeared into a dark hole. They followed it down the hole and have been pinched. The Yeti Crab refuses to let them go. That was months ago and I haven't heard from them since.

☎ Gone to see if Black Holes actually exist. They have been gone for sixteen years. What do you think?

☎ Gone to Kansas to count sunflower seeds. May take forever.

☎ Travelling the globe to give pedicures to all of the world's wild elephants. Not sure if they will make it home due to the high risk of being trampled. Please pray for them!

☎ Gone to investigate the Bermuda Triangle in hopes of finding all the missing people, planes and ships. They have been gone for 43 years. I am starting to get worried.

☎ Were inspired after buying a new pair of runners and went jogging – that was fifteen years ago and haven't come back.

☎ Gone to Newfoundland to hunt for the Great White Whale—hopefully they don't end up like Jonah!

☎ Gone to find Bill who is known for some sort of beans. Apparently he planted them and then never returned. It truly is a mystery. Just give me your number and I'll get them to call you back when they return from their adventure.

☎ Gone to the highest elevations of the world to find the best coffee bean farmers. Whenever she phones I cannot understand a word because she's so hyper and talks so fast – I think she might have a caffeine problem! I don't think she will ever return.

☎ Gone to find a needle in one of the world's biggest haystacks; once they find the needle they're going to sew curtains for every house in North America.

☎ Gone to play dueling banjos up in the Ozarks.

☎ Gone to Kananaskis country in Alberta to try and communicate with the bears there and see if they are concerned about bees not pollenating – reducing their food supply.

☎ Gone to Niagara Falls to attempt going over them in a barrel. Success rate doesn't look very good.

☎ Gone fishing using their bare hands, attempting to increase their agility.

☎ Went to Italy to make a very long noodle. Not expecting them back for a very long time.

☎ Gone to search for little people who live under colorful mushrooms. Yet, I believe that perhaps they have been eating the mushrooms and the little people have taken over their brains.

☎ Gone to develop a communications device that will replace the telephone – I heard mindreading mentioned. They said they should be finished in 5 years but that they wouldn't phone me until they could use their telepathic skills.

☎ Gone to recapture the sixties. They put on go-go boots and did the pony out the door. I don't think they are returning.

☎ Went to train as knife throwers for a circus act. They need volunteers to practice on – would you be interested?

☎ Gone to develop a musical act using termites. They want to see if they can stop the termites from eating the wooden instruments. They have spent the past 8 months trying to get them trained, to no avail. They keep having to replace the instruments. Don't expect them back for several years.

☎ Gone to test apples to see if they actually make you do bad things.

☎ Traipsing around the world with their alarm clock to see if time can travel. Will be gone for several months.

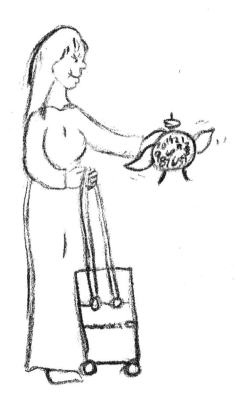

☎ Went to the Casino to win the big Jackpot. The last I heard from them they had locked their keys in the car and then sold it to a loan shark. I haven't heard from them in 4 days. I fear the worst.

☎ Gone to Transylvania to find Count Dracula. I have not heard from them in months and I think they might have been bitten. What do you think I should do? What if they return? Do you believe in vampires?

☎ Gone to Tasmania to look for the Tasmanian devil. To see if he spins as fast as he does in the cartoons, and if so, how does he do it?

☎ Gone ghost-hunting in Bannock, Montana. I don't know when they will be back – I fear they have been possessed!

☎ Gone to Rome to get exorcised – don't know if they will ever be back since the demons maybe too strong. I stay awake at night fearing what this could mean for us all. Please pray for them!

☎ Gone to find the place where minds achieve peace. Perhaps another planet? Don't expect them back!

☎ They built a time machine and said they were going to test it. That was a month ago. I can't believe it but it's possible that time travel actually exists.

☎ Gone to put cotton on swabs. Be back in their own cotton-pickin' time!

☎ Gone to study all the different faiths in every country of the world. They said that they are expecting to return in March 2062. I can leave them a message and get them to call you then.

☎ Went to go look for the extraordinary in the ordinary and don't know if or when they will ever return.

☎ Went to Japan to live on an island where the only inhabitants are rabbits. I believe it is called Bunny Island. The last letter I received from them was full of carrots and fur. I think the rabbits have taken them captive. I am not sure what I should do. Please help me.

☎ Gone to the beach to check the circumference of each sand particle, placing the good circumferences in one pail and the bad in another. Don't expect him to return for 100 years.

☎ Went to find a land that only grows flowers – they plan to call it Flower Land. Don't expect them ever to return home.

☎ They went to paint a white line around the world; they won't be back anytime soon unless they run out of paint.

☎ They went to play hopscotch on a rubber ball in Scotland – they are going to try and bounce themselves back to Canada. Not sure how long it will take.

☎ Went tobogganing down Mount Everest. They may be back – if they survive!

☎ Went to Ottawa to sell their invention which makes the deficit disappear. If it works, the government will keep them on as employees… alas, they shall never return!

☎ Went to Idaho to peel potatoes from every farm in the state. If they ever get done, the peelings will be used to build a car in which they will drive back to Canada. I believe it may take 22 years.

☎ Went to a newly discovered lake – supposedly the fish are able to talk! Maybe if they get phone service out there you can try to sell your product to the fish in the lake? What's your number so I can pass it on to the fish?

☎ Went to do research on what makes a telemarketer tick. Said he was going undercover to spy on every telemarketer's every move! After their research is done I believe they plan to write a pocketbook to prevent innocent people from being bothered at home by telemarketers; to teach them what to say and how to handle the nonstop nuisance. I despair of them ever returning!

Telemarketer
Be
Gone

TELEMARKETER BE GONE ! ! ! ! !

Thank you so much for reading our
guidebook.

I hope that you enjoyed it and that the
material was useful!

Take care out there, and always remember to
be kind to all!

For we are all one big family!